Sociopaths in Today's World
How They Hide in Plain Sight

By Michael Minsen

Introduction

I want to thank you and congratulate you for downloading the book, *"Sociopaths in Today's World: How They Hide in Plain Sight"*.

This book contains proven steps and strategies on how to know what sociopaths are, how different they are from you and me, and how you can identify their kind so you won't be a victim.

A sociopath is a person who lacks empathy and doesn't have remorse. He usually is conning, chronically manipulative and (almost always) dangerous. Most of the times, you'll find it difficult to be around this kind of person.

Would you know how to identify a sociopath if you see one? It's not as easy as it seems – sociopaths don't appear bad; they dress well, and are actually likeable when he wishes to be one.

There are minute differences and the terms are often interchanged, but don't be mistaken – a sociopath is different from a psychopath. Are you a sociopath or a psychopath?

Sociopaths are all around you. They can be one of your next door neighbors, classmates in school, or work colleagues. They're good in blending; they're planning the next steps on how they can pounce on their next prey.

Learn to expose sociopaths. Don't be their next victim. Instead, be one of those who are smart enough to avoid their cunning ways.

Thanks again for downloading this book, I hope you enjoy it!

Why You Should Read This Book

Sociopaths are all around you. They don't appear like the bad guys you see in movies. Sociopaths are dressed well, and have good manners. They're not always jailed and kept in prisons. They can be your next door neighbor or your pesky colleague.

It's best to find out all about sociopaths and understand how they mingle, blend, and hide so that you'll be afflicted with as less damage as possible.

Read this book. Don't be a victim.

Copyright

Disclaimer

The information provided in this book is designed to provide helpful information on the subjects discussed. This book is not meant to be used, nor should it be used, to diagnose or treat any medical condition. For diagnosis or treatment of any medical problem, consult your own physician. The publisher and author are not responsible for any specific health or allergy needs that may require medical supervision and are not liable for any damages or negative consequences from any treatment, action, application or preparation, to any person reading or following the information in this book. Any references included are provided for informational purposes only and do not constitute endorsement of any websites or other sources. Readers should be aware that any websites listed in this book may change.

Table of Contents

Chapter 1 – Uncovering the Sociopath

Who is a sociopath? Do you know someone who's a sociopath? Are you a sociopath?

How will you define the word 'sociopath'?

A **sociopath** is someone with Antisocial Personality Disorder who shows himself in extreme antisocial behavior and attitudes, as well as a lack of conscience. A sociopath has Antisocial Personality Disorder; they show a persistent pattern of disregard for other people's rights and feelings.

People having Antisocial Personality Disorder have a manner of thinking, relating to others and perceiving situations that are destructive and dysfunctional. They usually have no regard for what is right or wrong, and they often are inconsiderate of the rights, feelings and wishes of others.

Why is sociopathy fascinating? It's because of the mystery that surrounds it. You don't understand a lot about it. Overall, a sociopath is somehow misunderstood, and it shows mainly in the belief that a sociopath always wishes to harm other people.

Are sociopath really bad people? It's easy to respond a full-throated "yes" for quite a lot of reasons, but it's not because they intend to have these kinds of feelings toward other people. The problem with sociopaths is that they don't have any feelings for others; that's why they treat other people as objects. Their behaviors' effect is definitely malicious, even though they don't intend to be malicious.

BECOMING A SOCIOPATH

Are you born a sociopath? Or somehow, you're molded to be one?

The truth is, nobody really knows. There's no exact explanation on how someone becomes a sociopath.

Is it a chosen path? Or is it something you're born with?

There are two distinct theories on how a person becomes a sociopath, or how a person is diagnosed to be one.

Experts in mental health and psychology believe that there's something in a person's genetic content that determines whether he or she is sociopathic, or a learned behavior molded by experiences during childhood. It can come from neglectful or abusive parents or guardians.

Research indicates that about 50% of the sociopathy cause can be traced to heritability, and the remaining 50% is a mixture of different factors. So it's either genetic or environmental.

DETERMINATION AND DIAGNOSIS

There are different criteria for people to be diagnosed as a sociopath.

Here are some of them:

- The individual has to be at least 18 years old.
- The individual has to have shown disregard and has violated other people's rights since 15 years of age; these rights include the following:
  - Repeated assaults on other people
  - Committed acts repeatedly that could lead to arrest
  - Impulsive; doesn't feel the need to plan ahead
  - Deceives other people for profit or pleasure; tells lies repeatedly; uses aliases
  - Doesn't care about their or other people's safety
  - Exemplifies poor work behavior; fails to honor their financial obligations
  - Rationalizes the pain they impose on others
- Shows evidence of Conduct Disorders; onset should be prior to reaching 15 years of age
- Symptoms seen on the individual should not be because of a different mental disorder

It's hard to diagnose this condition because there are a lot of symptoms and variations that can take place. But still, it's possible to identify someone with this disorder.

Being diagnosed with sociopathy will mean a new path being opened. Is it the end? No. It's just the beginning. That's why it's best to recognize a person with sociopathy so you can protect not only yourself, but the person as well.

Chapter 2 – Sociopath Spotted

Who is a sociopath? Do you know someone who's a sociopath? Are you a sociopath?

A person described as a sociopath has various traits that differentiate them from people without personality disorders.

Sociopaths are experts in influencing and deceiving people. They might speak of things that are not truthful or realistic, but they still are skillful in making those things sound believable, even if they just made those things up.

A lot of people get scammed, hoodwinked or even harmed by sociopaths. If you're not too careful, you can get sucked into their influence.

Identify sociopaths. Avoid them. Save yourself from their cunning minds.

IDENTIFYING A SOCIOPATH

Sociopaths usually are highly intelligent. Rather than empowering people, sociopaths use their minds to deceive. Their intelligence is what makes them dangerous. If you'll notice, a lot of famous serial killers who were able to evade the law were sociopaths.

Sociopaths are charming. They contain high charisma; they tend to attract groups of people, mainly because people love to be around them and choose to be in their presence. They have this "glow", and this attracts people who need guidance or direction. Sociopaths usually appear sexy, or have this strong sex appeal. Obviously, not all sexy people are sociopaths, but be wary of those who have weird fetishes as well as outrageous sexual appetites.

Sociopaths are more intense and spontaneous compared to other people. You'll see them commit bizarre and even erratic things that normal people wouldn't easily do. They are not bound by the usual social contracts; you'll see them as people who are irrational and/or extremely risky.

Sociopaths speak poetically. They are masters in choosing the right words. They can deliver a monologue that runs a "stream of consciousness" that's both hypnotic and intriguing. They are expert poets and storytellers.

Sociopaths don't feel guilt, shame or remorse. Their minds just don't have the right circuitry to sort out such emotions. This mindset gives them the ability to threaten people, betray or even harm people without having second thoughts.

They engage in actions that will benefit them even if it results to the harm of other people.

Sociopaths are not capable of love. They are entirely self-serving. They may pretend compassion or love so they can get what they want, but it's not real love. Sociopaths can create relationships, but these are merely relationships in name. They can go ahead and end the relationship whenever it suits them or whenever they feel it necessary. Their relationships are without meaning or depth, and these include marriages.

Sociopaths don't apologize. They are always right. They don't feel guilty. They don't say sorry. You may show proof that they're wrong, but they still won't apologize and will attack you instead.

Sociopaths aim to dominate other people and are too competitive. They don't like losing to anything. They like to win and they love to dominate. Arguments, fights... name it, they'd aim to win it. They will create a web of lies if needed, and will go the extra mile just to viciously defend this web even risking logical absurdity.

Sociopaths tell lies about their experiences. They tend to exaggerate things, even reaching a point when it's already absurd. Their lies are narrated in a storytelling format, and for some reason their lies sound believable.

Sociopaths are caught in their own delusions; they believe that their words become the truth. According to them, their words are so powerful; whatever they utter takes place.

Sociopaths are unreliable and irresponsible. They are not concerned about wrecking other people's hopes and dreams. They are indifferent and oblivious to whatever devastation they cause. They don't feel accountable for their actions. They don't accept blame directed to themselves but to other people, even for those actions they committed themselves.

SPOT THEM FIRST

...before they see you. You have to identify easily observable traits or behaviors that are correlated well with sociopathy.

Here are some that you have to take note of:

- Sociopaths don't talk about themselves unless it's going to be used as a diversion or bait. They'll be driving the conversation to their acquaintance to gather information as much as they can.

- They'll only provide limited personal details – this is done only to give a false feeling of trust or intimacy. Revealing truths about them will happen rarely, and usually just slips of the tongue.

- Most of the time, sociopaths take time before responding. You won't easily understand if they are annoyed, bored, lying or all of the above.

- They don't provide reactions to sensitive social and political topics.

- They have monotone voices, and they seem different when they got "distracted".

- They tend to take things too literally; they also don't give appropriate responses to small emotional cues. They also don't appear embarrassed, and can win large crowds easily.

- They show cold indifference toward one or more members of the family.

You may manifest these signs but won't necessarily mean that you're already a sociopath. Being a sociopath, though, will mean you'll show these signs.

Chapter 3 – Sociopath or Psychopath

You can hear criminologists, psychologists and psychiatrists use the terms psychopathy and sociopathy interchangeably. Are you able to discern their individual qualities? Are you able to determine who is a sociopath, and who is a psychopath?

Sociopathy and psychopathy are both anti-social personality disorders. These two conditions are results of an interaction between environmental factors and genetic predispositions.

The term *sociopath* is used when the person's antisocial behavior is caused by belief system and upbringing, or a result of a brain injury. The term *psychopath* is used on the other hand if the underlying cause is leaning towards the hereditary. Recently, the latter has already acquired a particular meaning, and the condition is better understood.

UNDERSTANDING THE DIFFERENCES

Sociopaths have comparatively normal temperaments; the personality disorder is caused by negative sociological factors such as delinquent peers, parental neglect, poverty, and extremely high or extremely low intelligence.

Psychopaths are born possessing temperamental differences such as cortical under-arousal, impulsiveness, and fearlessness. These attitudes lead them to seek risks and unable to internalize social norms.

These personality disorders lead to extremely violent acts. Psychiatrists may view sociopaths and psychopaths as one and the same, but criminologists treat them differently due to the differences in their outward behavior.

Here's a chart that further illustrate their differences:

	SOCIOPATH	PSYCHOPATH
Suffers from:	Antisocial personality disorder (ASPD)	Antisocial personality disorder; delusional, lack of conscience or empathy
Origin of Illness:	environmental factors e.g. upbringing	hereditary i.e. nature part of the debate (nature vs. nurture

Predisposition to Violence	Varied	High
Behavior	Erratic	Controlled
Impulsivity	High	Usually low, but still varies
Criminal Predispositions	Has a tendency of having opportunistic or impulsive behavior / violence, excessive risk taking	Has a tendency for different premeditated crimes having controllable risks, fraud, opportunistic or calculated violence
Criminal Behavior	Leans toward leaving clues and acting on impulse	Leans to participate in schemes as well as take calculated risks in order to lessen exposure or evidence
Social Relationships	Can appear superficially normal towards social relationships; usually are social predators. Can empathize with family and friends; can still feel guilty after hurting loved ones	Can't maintain normal relationships. Only takes care of relationships that benefit themselves. Can hurt friends and family without getting hurt

DIFFERENCES IN THEIR OUTWARD BEHAVIOR

Career

Sociopaths usually find it difficult to maintain a home and a steady job.

Psychopaths on the other hand usually have successful careers and aim to make other people trust and like them. Psychopaths understand social emotions of humans quite well but can't experience them, and this makes them capable of manipulating human emotions.

Social Relationships

Both psychopaths and sociopaths are capable of creating relationships. Psychopaths' neurology makes it difficult for them to feel empathy. What they value are relationships in which they benefit from, but they don't feel guilty when they take advantage of their families and close friends.

Both sociopaths and psychopaths can be really charming, but it's more of sociopaths who can still feel empathy and guilt. This is the reason behind their relationships still capable of being 'normal'.

Psychopaths can be insidious and manipulative of the people around them. Unlike sociopaths, psychopaths can almost be too organized, and they can give the impression of being normal in the relationships they create, hence forming either symbiotic or parasitic relationships.

Violent Tendencies

Psychopathy may be linked to impulsiveness, but they are still very meticulous in planning their moves. For a long time, you won't be able to detect their crimes. It's rare that they'd do violent crimes; they'd more likely take advantage of people around them without having to resort to illegal acts, or commit white collar crime e.g. fraud.

Sociopaths' outbreaks of violence usually are unplanned and erratic. Sociopaths also are inclined to leave more clues.

Psychopaths and sociopaths both commit crime due to revenge or greed. Psychopaths however feel no remorse; this is because they don't have the ability to empathize.

SIMILARITIES OF SOCIOPATHS AND PSYCHOPATHS

Both psychopaths and sociopaths possess medical disorders that can be alleviated or treated if diagnosed properly. Treatment for the said conditions may involve therapies and/or proper medication.

Psychiatrists don't determine the condition based on behavior; what they do is base the condition on its origin. A person is diagnosed a psychopath if his/her state is mainly congenital, and a person is diagnosed a sociopath if his/her state is caused by social conditions such as abuse during childhood.

Both cases' symptoms start to establish and come out when the person is around fifteen years old.

The first symptom exhibited is usually excessive animal cruelty, afterwards, there's the lack of conscience, guilt or remorse for hurtful actions to other people at a later stage. The sociopath might have understood the proper social behavior but does not express any emotional responses to other people's actions. Psychopaths won't be able to form genuine relationships, and may show reactions that are out of proportion to perceived negligence.

Bear in mind that psychopaths are different from psychotics; psychopaths are not mentally disabled, and don't lose their contact with reality. Psychotic people suffer breaks from reality, and they are characterized by hallucinations and delusions, hence don't function normally.

Chapter 4 – Types of Sociopaths

Sociopaths have the same general traits, but they are all different, like the rest of the society. Some are violent, and some are not. Some cheat, and some don't. All display controlling attitudes. All manipulate and tell lies. All can be deceptive. All are interested and self-motivated.

There are different types of sociopaths. Usually, what makes the difference is not what's inside their heads, but what's inside their hearts.

SOCIOPATHY DIVISIONS

Sociopathy is said to be divided into two: entitled and amoral.

Entitled Sociopath

An entitled sociopath can be either because of genes or the environment. It's wherein the sociopath is in a state of over entitlement, and his self needs validate any ends.

This type of sociopath doesn't have any ideals, and doesn't feel any shame in his or her actions. This sociopath type often feels satisfaction is what he or she does.

A lot of them enjoy mocking authority, and even be proud of it.

Amoral Sociopath

People who belong in this sociopath type don't have a sense of morality. This inexistence can lead to actions done without any sense of remorse, guilt and awareness of moral structures.

This is seen as a developmental state; the attention deficit disorder felt in childhood results into sociopathy with a weak awareness of pain conditions. They have primitive senses of self. They possibly won't have any acknowledgement, have right boundaries or distinction, or recognize others' pain.

This could have been caused by not having compassionate caregivers. With this lack of care, they gain the ability to not feel others' pain and be satisfied with getting what they wish for.

SOCIOPATH CLASSIFICATIONS

Aside from the two divisions of sociopathy, there are other classifications to describe sociopaths better.

Common Sociopaths

Oftentimes called subcultural delinquents, the common sociopaths are those who make up most of sociopathic personality disorders. They don't always use their conscience to make decisions that could affect other people.

They seem to increase in number due to higher instances of incompetent parenting. Their conscience is unelaborated and weak; they don't get shamed of things that would normally shame other individuals. Instead of being happy with observing rules, they take pride in breaking rules. They are not happy with long-term goals.

Common sociopaths seem to travel all the time: they're either living in shelters or running away. They also seem to be prideful with regard to their anti-authoritative nature. They become feral creatures and stowaways. Regardless of their current situation, they appear to be happy with their lives and avoid responsibility for their actions.

Alienated Type

This type of sociopath has problems with empathy toward other individuals. They are not capable of feeling connections or emotional intimacy to other people. They can't contain violent urges and they commit criminal behavior. Some of them, though, are still capable of showing feelings toward pets or objects.

Being an alienated sociopath could have been due to genetics, or because of an unloving environment during childhood. Their symptoms include irresponsibility, manipulation, exaggerated sexuality and refusal to follow societal norms.

There are different types of alienated sociopaths:

a. Disaffiliated Type

The person with this type is not able to connect to other people in every aspect of his life. All his connections and relationships are twisted with lack of intimacy.

Research shows that this kind of sociopath is caused by the lack of nurture and care; this contributed to the sociopath's underdevelopment of attachment and love.

b. Disempathic Type

This individual is still able of investing emotions to a limited group, and this group can include pets, friends or family members. Those who are not included in this group are seen as objects.

Human beings are capable of empathy, and they can share to an extent joy and pain of other human beings. However, this capability still has to be developed through experience.

There are also individual differences in what can be included in a sociopath's circle of empathy. One can share pain of animals and hate hunters, and one can feel the other way around.

c. Hostile Type

This sociopath type is always violent, angry and aggressive. They always feel rejected by society and they think they won't be able to succeed because of the set rules.

People may hoard grievances and develop a type of chronic irritability as they get older; when one gets irritated, he feels stronger and more puissant.

They stop themselves from being sad and depressed by using their anger as their means of survival mechanism. They adopt a destructive attitude; they feel being angry is more acceptable compared to being sad, frightened and depressed.

d. Cheated Type

The cheated sociopath feels deprived in life due to some uncontrollable circumstances – maybe an unattractive appearance or a physical disability. They may also feel disadvantaged because of minority status, or social or class origin.

Because of this "deprived" feeling, they tend to disobey the rules of society; they believe they've been cheated of a good life. Since they feel cheated, the rules will no longer apply to them. They think they don't have to justify their conduct.

Aggressive Sociopath

To get their way, aggressive sociopaths utilize frightening, hurting and tyrannizing other people. From it, they derive feelings of power and importance.

Sociopaths in this group usually become muggers, rapists, and other violent criminals who state that they get a lot of gratification from dominance and control over their prey.

People who are tough, bold, unflinching and brash are admired in the streets, and such behavior is reinforced. Usually aggressive and muscular males take this course to become the ultimate Alpha Male.

Dissocial Sociopath

Dissocial sociopaths are those who are normal (that's both psychologically and temperamentally), but their identification and allegiance is with a subculture with norms and mores that have opposing views to the other cultures.

Usually dissocial sociopaths become the members of political underground movements or terrorist groups. They can also become boys in street gangs who honor rules, but the wrong rules.

Chapter 5 – Blending In

If you think sociopaths have this crazy and sinister appearance, then it's time to change your outlook. If your idea of a sociopath is that of Ted Bundy and Hannibal Lecter, then sadly, you're mistaken.

Serial killers are all sociopaths. Not all sociopaths, however, are serial killers.

You may have crossed paths with a sociopath, and you may have not known it. That's how skilled a sociopath is in blending in.

Learn how sociopaths mingle with people.

Looks Can Deceive

Sociopaths look average. They're non-descript. They can be attractive. They can be entertaining, charming and witty – just like anybody else. You'd think that bad people look *bad*, but sociopaths don't appear in such manner.

There are sociopaths from all walks of life. There are sociopaths who are from well-educated and well-off families. There are some who have good social graces. They are capable of dressing well, and they can behave well in polite society.

This 'camouflage' doesn't hinder them from cheating, lying and stealing, though. It even makes deceiving easier for them. Those sociopaths who come from middle-class or privileged families usually excel in committing white collar crimes such as phony stock schemes, fraud and embezzlement.

Uses a Lot of Tools

Sociopaths are capable of using a lot of tools. They are too charming; their charisma is almost animal-like. They have this affinity to danger. They are spontaneous and have magnetic personalities. They give people around them this feeling of familiarity. Intimacy is established quickly. Seduction is used when necessary.

"We" statements are used by sociopaths. They start distractions with their professional and social roles, whether they become a humanitarian, benefactor or animal lover. They are into gaslighting – they make you doubt your views of reality.

Difficulty in Detection

Sociopaths are hard to recognize because of different reasons. One of which is because of them being fluent talkers i.e. liars. They might get caught in a lie, but they can easily change their stories without missing a beat. They're cool under pressure and are comfortable during social situations.

Sociopaths can also appear legitimate by using their family members and business connections. They can be – or pretend to be – lawyers, clergy, teachers, artists and counselors, so that they can easily be trusted by people. By appearing credible to most, people won't bother checking their credentials. If time comes that their credentials are needed, then they'd be more than willing to fabricate and even exaggerate their credentials.

Gaining Your Trust

To gain your trust, they'll tell you the words you want to hear, whether it's "you can trust me", "I won't do it again", or even "I love you". It'll mean nothing to them, but if it'll give them what they want, then they won't hesitate to do so.

They can blend inconspicuously with everybody, and unless you're scrutinizing their behavior, you won't realize that something's amiss. Maybe you won't even notice.

They are skilled con artists. It will be very hard to determine whether your office co-worker or quiet neighbor is a sociopath. They can imitate reactions and behaviors of people who are more empathic and know better how to gain others' trust.

Chapter 6 – Exposure and Defense

Sociopaths bring chaos in people's lives through quiet means. That's how most sociopaths work.

You may have known someone who had left you devastated, chilled, or confused – or maybe all at the same time. Perhaps you've been involved romantically with someone whom you now describe as 'evil'. You may have worked with a boss you refer to now as 'psycho'. You may have had a domineering neighbor who seemed to check out on all the things you do.

Most sociopaths don't kill. They don't take lives. They make your life miserable. What they take is your happiness.

Isn't it great to spot a sociopath before they wreak havoc into your life?

To stop a sociopath in his or her tracks, you have to expose them and let them know that you know what they're up to.

Fact Checking

A simple method you can use to dispel sociopathic delusion is to begin fact checking their claims. Do any of their stated claims actually have basis and actually check out?

Start digging – upon doing so, you'll see a pattern of repeated inconsistencies.

If it's a sane person you confront, he'll just be happy to clarify the misunderstandings and misinformation. But if it's a sociopath that you confront and let them know of the inconsistency, they'll be aggressive or angry and feel that you doubt their integrity.

Don't fact check the sociopath by asking those who are under the sociopath's influence. A sociopath usually has a group of people who believes their fictional stories, and this group actually internalizes those stories to the point that memories are already created to make the stories more real.

For example, a guru-style sociopath repeatedly discusses his levitation stories. His believers will then soon create false memories and believe that he actually did it. Ask his believers if he did levitate, and the believers will definitely say 'yes' because in their minds, there is an illusion created of him levitating.

The same scenario also can be applied to sociopathic politicians. They may claim that they've created 'millions of jobs' even if they didn't. His followers on the other hand will repeat the lie and proclaim the jobs he had created.

This is why you should always need evidence that won't come within his circle of influence. If what he says doesn't check out outside of his circle of influence, then he might be a sociopath.

Get Professional Help

Yes, it's the sociopath who has mental issues but if you've had encounters with a sociopath, it will also help to seek medical assistance.

You can talk to a therapist who will enlighten you about the steps taken by the sociopath to charm and manipulate you. Why does this matter? Two things: one, it helps you view the relationship clearly, and two, it will remove the power that the sociopath has placed over you.

Sociopaths love domination. Once it becomes clear that they have to exert more effort to take over your head, then they'll loosen their grip and eventually will let you go... and look for another willing victim.

Avoiding a Sociopath

Sociopaths are all violent. Some are emotionally violent, while some are physically violent as well.

Here are some indicators of sociopathy that may seem like a list of sociopathic characteristics:

- *Speaks in "we" terms*, such as "We don't have to do this."

- *Forced teaming*, wherein the person makes you feel the two of you have something in common, even though there isn't anything you both share

- *Shares too many details,* wherein the sociopath adds excessive details to make themselves more believable and credible, especially when they're lying.

- *Charm and niceness*, wherein the sociopath is polite and friendly to his victims so he can manipulate them and/or to disarm their mistrust.

- *Loan sharking,* wherein he gives unsolicited help to his chosen victim, and he anticipates the other person to feel obliged to provide reciprocal openness in return.

- *Typecasting,* when the sociopath gives an insult to a selected victim who would most likely fall into a conversation to counteract the said insult. The sociopath uses the conversation as a trap for the victim.

- *Providing unsolicited promises*, i.e. making promises to do things even when the promise is not asked for, or the other way around. This means that the uttered promise will usually be broken.

- *The word 'no' is discounted*, which means the sociopath refuses to accept rejection. The victim might say no, but the sociopath won't accept it and will insist their way.

Now, you have at least an idea on what a sociopath might be like or might do. It should help you a lot in recognizing a sociopath, and red flags should now rise when you cross paths with one. Save yourself – avoid sociopaths at all costs.

Bonus Chapter – Famous Sociopaths

To help you understand the concept of sociopathy further, here are some famous sociopaths who you can use to study for better understanding of their behavior.

REAL LIFE SOCIOPATHS

Charles Manson

Charles Manson was a quasi-commune who lived in California during the 60s. He was convicted of conspiracy to the Tate/LaBianca murders. He was not found guilty of being the one who did wherein all the actions were done according to his instructions.

He was described as one who suffered from instability, rejection and psychic trauma, as well as always in need of status and assurance of love.

His actions were the inspiration for the book Helter Skelter. He's associated with brutal slayings, and his famous 'mad eyes' are still used today in news stories. He was again denied parole in May 2007.

L. Ron Hubbard

Lafayette Ron Hubbard, also referred to as L. Ron Hubbard or sometimes LRH, is a drug fiend and a science fiction writer who took part in an ultimate experiment: to establish a religion founded on entire crap, but still containing the psychological and sociological components needed to make it successful.

He was a mediocre writer but was still successful in writing Dianetics, which proved how gullible people can be. His fame is also attributed to the religion he created which is Scientology, which has followers – and still continues to gain millions of followers.

Elizabeth Bathory

Countess Elizabeth Bathory de Ecsed has been labeled as history's most prolific serial killer, though the actual number of her victims is still to be confirmed. She along with four other collaborators were accused to have tortured and killed hundreds of girls from years 1585 to 1610.

The details of the brutality and serial murders were verified by given testimonies of about 300 witnesses and survivors, and physical evidence plus the presence of mutilated dying, imprisoned and dead girls were found when she was arrested. She was said to have vampire-like tendencies, and the stories were documented years after she passed on.

Ted Bundy

Ted Bundy is one of the most famous sociopaths. His crimes are well-known – he chose random women and brutally beat, raped and strangled them to their death. After that, he went back to the scene of the crime, and had sex with the mutilated bodies. Yes, that's one of his better days.

For Bundy, women were toys. They were attractive targets.

He knew he was a wild animal. He felt no remorse. He always lied about his crimes even though there were a lot of evidence. He confessed a few times but always mentioned that those were only out of desperation. Still, nobody can deny that he enjoyed himself and did what he wished to control society.

POP CULTURE SOCIOPATHS

Movies and television shows both have their own share of depicting sociopaths.

Alex Delarge (*A Clockwork Orange*)

He's attractive. He stands out even in futuristic London. He has a glorious fashion sense and has great taste in music. His favorite composer is even Ludwig Van.

He might seem normal enough – likeable, even. He can be too charming when he wishes to be. You can't trust him, though. He's violent, and is associated with rape and murder.

Dr. Hannibal Lecter (*Silence of the Lambs*)

Hannibal Lecter is a well-educated person who knows good music when he hears one. His voice is incredibly soothing, and is most likely at the top of the most polite serial killers.

Too good, is he, right? But no. He eats people. He follows them around, calls them, and when he talks to them, he makes slurping sounds. He also wears a mask plus a straightjacket.

The Joker (*The Dark Knight*)

He's entertaining and extremely intriguing. He's messed up – if it's because of an abusive father or a wife who was attacked by vicious loan sharks, you won't know. You know how the Joker is; you don't really know when he's serious.

How messed up is he? He's frightening. His mission is to annihilate society, as everything's simply a big joke. Doesn't his face paint scare you? Well, it should.

Dexter (*Dexter*)

Dexter doesn't feel real emotions. He kills people, yes, but his victims are those who won't affect you that much, so maybe that's why you're quite comfortable with the killings. He's a sociopath who somehow changed to become a little bit of a psycho schizophrenic.

Dexter kills people, and plays God by choosing whose lives to take next. He could snap anytime, and his 'dark passenger' could take over anytime, and that makes things scary. He admits to faking interactions, and he knows he can fake them well.

Patrick Bateman (*American Psycho*)

You'll love him for his exquisite taste – he's expert on things that are beauty or culture-related, whether it's business cards, fine dining, music or skin care.

Why shouldn't you love him? For one, he's an axe-welding murderous psycho who mutilates bodies.

Conclusion

Now that you're aware of what sociopaths are, how they came to be and what they do, what are you going to do next?

The next step is to apply what you've learned. Be more wary of your surroundings. If you see something suspicious, then follow your instincts. Bear in mind that sociopaths can be so cunning and manipulative.

Read books (like what you're holding now) that deal with mind control. Watch movies and videos to see what happened. Apply what you've seen, and see yourself break free from the influence of the sociopath.

If you've been a victim of a sociopath, then don't be afraid. Lessons were learned and you know how to be careful in the future. It's never your fault. A person was deliberately changing your reality, controlling your behavior and influencing your decisions. You didn't know what was going on. Forgive yourself.

Still have doubts? Well, the victims of these sociopaths didn't think there was something wrong, either.

Good thing you have this book. Be safe than sorry.

One Last Thing...

If you enjoyed this book or found it useful I'd be very grateful if you'd post a short review on Amazon. Your support really does make a difference and I read all the reviews personally so I can get your feedback and make this book even better.

If you'd like to leave a review then all you need to do is click the review link on this book's page...

Thank You so Much